EVERYTHING WE THINK WE HEAR

JOSÉ ÁNGEL

ARAGUZ

FLORICANTO PRESS

Copyright © 2015 by José Ángel Araguz

Copyright © 2015 of this edition by Floricanto™ Press and Berkeley Press

All rights reserved. No part of this publication may be stored in a retrieval system, transmitted or reproduced in any way, including but not limited to photocopy, photograph, magnetic, laser or other type of record, without prior agreement and written permission of the publisher.

Floricanto is a trademark of Floricanto Press.

Berkeley Press is an imprint of Inter-American Development, Inc.

FLORICANTO™ PRESS

7177 Walnut Canyon Rd.

Moorpark, California 93021

(415) 793-2662

www. FLORICANTOPRESS. com

ISBN-13: 978-1518644917

"Por nuestra cultura hablarán nuestros libros. Our books shall speak for our culture."
Roberto Cabello-Argandoña, Editor

EVERYTHING

para Adelita: *¿Qué piensas?*

TABLE OF CONTENTS

Section one   **11**

Directions   13

Directives and Secrets   14

Spiderman Hitches a Ride   15

Love Dream   17

Walks   18

Don't Look Now I Might Be Mexican   19

Throwing Myself in   20

Drinking at Home   21

Forgotten Conversation   23

Childhood   24

The Boy Who Could Not Dream   25

Bombs   26

In Case of Omission   28

Figure   29

5 a.m.   30

Section two   31

Mass Transit   33
Concrete   35
Verisimilitude   36
Jalapeños   37
Dispatch from the Knight Called
    Friday Night   38
Morning Communion   39
How   40
Zoot Suit Riot   41
Stream   42
Taken   44
Ocean Dream   45
Bukowski   46
My History with the
    Spanish Language   47
Raro   48

Section three   **51**

Old Love   53

Degas   54

Sky Stone   56

Books   57

Holiday Policy   59

Birthdays   60

Semblance   62

My *Tía*'s Throw   63

Letter to Rainer Maria Rilke

    from NYC   65

Ready   66

Traffic   68

Song   69

Slowed   70

Don't Shoot Me   71

Moth Season   73

Notes   **79**

Acknowledgments   81

10

Section one

12

Directions

The man asking for directions sighs when I answer him in Spanish, shakes my hand, almost hugs me. He tells me I look more Puerto Rican than Mexican but are we not all *hermanos, primos,* and maybe that is why I excuse him like a brother or a cousin when he points to my books and asks what I am studying and hears *la policía*. Before I can correct him, he releases another sigh and says alright, says he knew he could trust me when he saw me, says that is the best thing for a man, to be strong, to stand for something, that in this country it is like money to be a police officer: the girls love it, family approves, and your boys know they can trust you. As he goes on about parking tickets and handcuffs, I think about all the nice things being said and whether he would say them about *la poesía* and how the thing I do study is made up of everything we think we hear.

Directives and Secrets

My childhood is a book made up of directives and secrets: *enter*/a mouse gnawed on your tortilla before you got to the table that morning, not her: *watch your step*/he wanted to steal you from me, she thinks again and again, looking down at you in her arms: *read carefully*/between the pages of the Old Testament tucked under the spare tire in the trunk of her car, the last letter from your father to her: *fill in every blank*/he wrote songs to her on bandanas she left behind with the pair of white school shoes, they wouldn't fit: *sign at the bottom*/the man didn't think she was a prostitute, her friend said she was, she slapped him, slapped them both, made her way through the new city to feed you again a mix of water and sugar in your bottle, all she had: *listen closely*/summers spent alone eating mayonnaise sandwiches, you will remember the sound of keys rustled at the door, like another heart: *yield*/when you got heavy, she thought of letting you float on the river, the sky carried on your eyes: *tell no one*/one day I will come across the book again on a shelf, will turn its pages, know by the way it grows warm in my hands, like a face, that it is mine.

Spiderman Hitches a Ride

My mother compares me to Spiderman, and for a second I like it.

I mean, it's what I've always wanted: to be viewed in the glory of courage and costume; to be super tough and just, a city like a little brother needing me to battle bullies and take back lunch money, a villain defining me by default as a hero, his crooked eyebrows and overheated plans carnival mirror to my calm and valiant stance; to push out of paper bag clothes; to leave my shoes untied, their mouths open in awe; to slip on the muscles and dreams of tomorrow's headlines; to leave a woman breathless, with a single kiss amazed, her heart pounding at the thought of being in love with a man – in tights – who leaves her without a name or number with which to follow him into the fire.

He is like me, my mother says, because he too wants to do good things for people, but he gets beat up, can't find a job and his girl ends up dating someone else. He saves people's lives but is always *flaco y vago*, vagabond skinny with luck and life.

Is this what it meant for her when at seventeen I boarded a plane and soared out of this city, where if she couldn't see into my head she could at least put a roof over it? Those years I disappeared into the phone, and was *ok* in Santa Fe, *ok* in San Diego, *ok* in New York but still short and small in words.

M'ijo, no te preocupes, don't worry. She smiles, then slips off her seatbelt to reach over and wrap an arm around my neck, the other dropping a twenty into my lap. The green paper is wrinkled in waves that shudder and blur as I blink fast, trying once again to be heroic.

Love Dream

In which hail racks against the roof of my car, I am driving down the slack of a mountain, a valley of silver light widening before me.

The skyline is a woman's face.

Walks

Summer morning cracks in the water of the Ohio.

There are walks to work I can still feel in some part of my memory, which is a place not exactly the body, an elsewhere. I remember the lights and wide streets of Times Square, the darker stretch past Bryant Park, Grand Central Station in a 5 a.m. orange glow. I remember, too, thinking as I walked, that the Hudson and the East Rivers were elsewhere coursing, keeping different hours. Nowhere in these thoughts the cracks I missed, or didn't. Nowhere the missteps. Only the shifts in the body.

Walking makes you wise, a woman in Oregon said to me as we worked, walked the same narrow paths around counters, to tables, from tables to backroom. Miles of taking orders, of cleaning, of reminding ourselves to breathe, of the now underfoot passing under breath. Elsewhere, the Willamette. Elsewhere the Rio Grande.

> elsewhere
> my child's face
> reflecting past the sky

Don't Look Now I Might be Mexican

That was the title of the book in my dream. I was on the cover, black hair slicked back into grooves, like a record with sunlight needling off. The Mexican flag laid across my chest in a slant, slung over my shoulder like I had won a contest. I had on a blue blazer, khaki slacks and yellow shoes. I hear the Colombian girl I work with say: *You look dressed to ask for a loan. Ready to get that taco truck?* No, I am here to tell people about eighteen wheelers, families as cargo, caught, stunned to have to go back. *¿Qué te crees?* I want to tell about La Llorona by the side of a river so distraught from losing her child she became a myth. *Why the banana shoes then?* Not banana: my feet are the color between stop and go. *Is that why you're not smiling?* I look back at the photo, see my head hanging over the green, white and red. Is it shame or defeat that radiates like sunlight at my feet? I could be La Malinche. I could be my father with a son he threw into the ocean. I could be my mother with a son of postcards and phone calls. Did I say it right or are those shoes made of straw, am I to be heretic in this crusade of borders and kin? *Your ghosts are women crying over dead children? Isn't that everyone?* I tell her there is no river deep enough to slake the thirst of a land too dry for neighbors. She laughs. *It's raining, it's always raining. When rain hits a river, all it does is disappear.*

Throwing Myself In

The way to read a fairy tale is to throw yourself in.

– W. H. Auden

Were the story of my mother and father a fairytale, I would be what is left after the prince cleared his way to the sleeping beauty, kissed her, and stood there, both looking into each other's eyes a moment, before looking around at shaking walls and rising dust, whatever words between them lost in the sound of crumbling and falling.

I wouldn't be the world my mother knew brought down around her. Wouldn't be the world my father saw as a bramble he could help escape from, suddenly a trap. Wouldn't be the lifting of a curse become the lifting of what held one world, one life, together, without which life cannot go on the same.

I would be a part of each of them as they stood helpless, not knowing what to do. I would be the last thing seen, the beginning of a ruin made from each other.

Drinking at Home

Tonight, bent in bottle-gleam, I see the man I am.

My mother's brown eyes test me. Those: *No tuve nada* eyes. Those: *Yo te di todo* eyes. I drink her beer. She offered, and I told her no. She said to be polite, and polite becomes an arrow I know will ride the air most of the night, because conversations when we drink go everywhere.

She asks, and I say it is ok to drink as an escape. I don't tell her that to escape is to make it so you don't come back. We take turns not coming back.

Each pull bends our faces: the mother of dresses with flowers stitched down the front, garden of a mother on her way to work, becomes the anchor of a mother who fell to bed long after I had gone to sleep those nights where I was small enough to share a bed and float close to her shore. Another pull and again I am the child pretending to be asleep, holding a sheet over my head as my mother argues on the phone with a man.

These waters move the moon between us.

Instead of writing about her, I want to buy her a mansion, a car, a high school education. But I am always broke, educated enough to know the debts I owe. I eat her food, stretch what cash she sneaks into my hand like afternoon shadows, and hope one job will call, one word will spark God to whisper into my ear how to make these words mansion enough.

Until then, the arrow hits, and the waters fall from our brown eyes again, as if to fill these bottles.

Forgotten Conversation

I remember starting the book I borrowed – stole – a year earlier, since it was around me more than she was. Back then, I had the nights before me to call and call. 3AM, the back of my throat thick and smoke hollow, my tongue lingering over my R's:

Querrrida, sorry to call late, I'm here, one hundred three perrrrrcent chulo, you should call me. I have your Sandra Cisneros book, y como élla, I want you, juntito a mi.

When she didn't answer, I'd flip through the pages and marvel at the smell of cinnamon. I'd imagine an altar – perhaps candles and photographs around a night stand—her asleep, her son with the spiked collar and black boots replacing her black nail polish.

Back then, I had the nights before me full of perhaps. I would hold the book for hours, determined to get into it, the heart of a Mexican woman. Cisneros would've done it differently. She'd have a cigar and call herself Daddy. Her black hair would shine like plums in the moonlight as she prayed, unlike me, for something deeper than forgiveness.

If given a second chance, she'd get it right and steal love.

Childhood

Only at night had he been able to imagine love.

On the floor, tucked into a sleeping bag, warm and free of any sense of how big and clumsy he would become, snug and simple as a seed at the core of a fruit, pocketed away in the mouth of everything he could be capable of, he turned over on himself until he fell against the stars.

The Boy Who Could Not Dream

He grew up listening to others go on about doing things that in his inexperience seemed amazing. When he asked when they had done these things, they laughed at him, and said the word that mocked him ever since he first had it explained that when people sleep they dream.

Simple, only when he would lie in the dark and wait – asking himself: *is this a dream, this night, this ceiling, this silver taste in my mouth, is this dreaming* – he would only wake up hurt and exhausted.

He decided after a while not to believe anything people said unless he saw it in person – anything else was lies.

Then she kissed him.

No one believed him when he said it.

Having no way to prove it, he was not surprised when they beat him for spreading rumors. The whole time he was on the ground he was torn inside: *Have I been kissed – yes, I feel it still – but they tell me it is lies – is this blood, this pain, this rust in my mouth, is this dreaming?*

Bombs

On the television there is talk of two hundred casualties.

My youngest brothers pitch their limbs against the walls, push on the sofa, cannonball to their knees. My mother's head sinks into cushion – she has fallen asleep writing checks.

Children against brick walls do not pray, only try to remember their names.

Little boys break like bombs, their voices of siren whistle and laughter of rolling rocks. A pen strolls across my mother's lap, streaks her white shirt with a black lightning, her eyelids twitch.

A soldier with a mic at his chin looks down as if he had spilt his words and was trying to pick out what he had to say from the ground.

The lights of a truck at the window flicker to shadow on my skin. I run my brothers to their room. Pitched on her side, feet flat on the floor, my mother does not hear the copper of her unzipped purse mouthing a wide, dark word.

When I hear the grit of a key shoved into the doorknob, the pop and crack as it turns, I hope it is surrender. I hope it is two hundred people resurrected and wanting to spend the night. I hope it is my mother twelve years ago, hair permed and heavy on her neck, full make-up and a Saturday dress and heels, come back to ask:

You sure I look alright? I am meeting a man of millions who owns a furniture store, that's good, right? I mean, I look good? No more mayonnaise sandwiches after tonight, m'ijo, only steak, only the best, you and me, and a man who knows nothing about cowboy hats or loaded guns.

In case of omission

Wanting Buddha's name recited a hundred times, rosaries were made with a hundred and eight beads, the extra there in case of omission, which is not exactly a judgment on human weakness seeing as the string that holds the beads together (and stands for the penetrating power of all the Buddhas) is made of human hair.

Figure

Looking at a leaf – transparent except for the copy of the tree, the branches, the reaching out for the sky remade in the body so light between my fingers – I think of how my father disappeared and I have had to trace a figure of him inside myself, and how this figure goes on as long as I do.

5 A.M.

A look my father might have given had he the chance to come across my face again flashes in the eyes of the man being let out of the jail across the street from where I now work.

Through the fog, questions rise in the silence of the breaking sun.

Section two

32

Mass Transit

I learned I was a pervert watching two total strangers meet in Denver on their way to Colorado Springs. One smooth conversation and they were on each other all hands and slick fingers, she liked it so much her breast spilled out of her blouse.

I learned I wanted to be free listening to an elderly Mexican couple talk about family, Juarez and careless coyotes who count the money twice before taking off but forget to fill up the tanks of their trucks. The way blankets get eaten by starving, heat-stricken children. The way their son looked like a shaved goat when they found him.

I learned I hated being a man listening to a man talk about his territory, a small town in the desert where only twelve people lived. How he would take high school girls out there in his '67 Chevy convertible, get them drunk and dreamy-eyed staring at the stars. *I swear you can see'em all if you drive out far enough*, he said. Breath growing heavy, pupils twitching in wide eyes, expecting me to understand. The way threats work. The way the girl would stop screaming after a while.

I don't know how long I watched him spit shells, watched them hit the ground, round gobs of spit, backwash eyes with black and yellow irises that looked like clipped toenails, plucked eyelashes, or any other thing one can leave behind sliding across the floor at the feet of others as they sleep in seats that tremble like cold hands, the miles growing by the second between who we are and who we were.

Maybe it's the shifting scenery or the way the hours pass in blinks, lost in dust motes and engine hum. Somehow you forget how to be a person.

Concrete

Now I'm as old as my father was/ When less than a year was left him.

– Carl Dennis

At my age, my father had been in jail long enough to be accustomed to concrete, his walls, floors, and sky concrete. The same color as the memories I have of him. A color that does not deepen despite the ink and pages. A color that comes out in the weather only when the clouds are full and waiting to let fall nothing one can hold onto.

Verisimilitude

The Irish tell of a woman so beautiful the rain fell on the leaves of a bush where a blind man took shelter and began speaking to him of her, so that when he later sang of her everyone was convinced he had seen her, while all he could recall was the cold smell of roots and the sound of water.

Jalapeños

Pickled, you gleam, a smile hiding its teeth. Photo negative from Picture Day, money missing from my pockets, that smile. I can live without money; without food, I'm useless. Hunger is a tide: I walk down when it is low and see more. Over time, you've taught me to fashion sensibilities after what I can tolerate. When I am old and gray, and have eaten enough, I will tolerate everyone. When your darkness first cracked, did everyone go silent as you spilled out your many, tiny moons? And did he think himself a sky, the first to place your moons upon his tongue? Or was it only later, after biting into your body, thinking his own body turned water that the first looked down and found, piled in his hand, the dunes of ellipsis you keep inside? You are commas, keep each bite separate. You are semicolons, a tip of the hat to greet the day. Shape suggestive of the J in my name. Shape suggestive, period. My aunt threatening with you if I ever cussed. Sting of *I should've known better than to*. Without you, I am useless. Corpus Christi Bay begins to glisten with you. You keep riding on the color of the waves, mocking, many and mocking. Family pickled. Family sharp with vinegar. Family broken with bites. Hunger is a tide: when it is high, I remember I cannot swim. Through skin and seed, my filthy existence resumes, after the sting.

Dispatch from the Knight Called Friday Night

I remember holding a beer bottle to my chest and trying to play it like a guitar. What are men drinking, dancing with teeth bared? How did the night get to taste so thick with smoke and laughter? Why does my tongue swell at the thought of a woman walking away? Why do her steps sound like loose change? I remember leaning into a payphone, crying to a girl who can't love me or leave me enough. I remember lying flat on the sidewalk and thinking of my brothers who are not old enough to understand that when I say love it is not what they are asked to give to God in their prayers but rather how warm their beds are that is the cup of my howl. This just in: Love, I want to be mumbled off your lips, to crumble and collect on your chest. Seriously, I can play Beethoven on this thing, just give me a chance. I remember a dial tone blaring; whoever might've been listening has stopped. I hope I pissed them off. I remember holding a phone to my chest like children hold hands over their hearts during the Pledge of Allegiance. No one here is asking for my loyalty, yet I think I'd stand here even if I wasn't poor, empty or mad. Seriously, I can play "Freebird" on this thing, just give me a chance. What are men crying, laughing with teeth bared? I remember staring the night down until it became a forked path leading straight into the furnace of the dawn.

Morning Communion

With the woman who drives around the park emptying trash cans and watering the hanging plants, cleaning and clearing; between what is thrown away and what dies in the dark she lives. When the city rumbles awake and people finish unmaking their beds, this woman has made the park, shifted into place the context of walks, of cutting through, of what is simply glanced at in passing.

With the woman who cleans the salon every morning, I pass by and she is vacuuming, sweeping, walking by mirrors she never stops to look at her face flowering briefly and vanishing in her work.

With the man who sleeps on the street corner lying on a man-hole cover each night, who this morning is gone and in his place is steam rising from the holes in the cover lifting to the air in threads of light.

How

To the cop who for no reason turns to me at work and asks
me not to be an asshole, tells me he'll make life difficult, no matter,
curb or café, brown is brown, partner beside him laughing:

How should I explain to him that I am also a man?

Zoot-Suit Riot

Had the chains on the pocket watches been any longer, one would have seen men swinging from lamp posts by a moonstruck thread.

Stream

Against the railing of a subway entrance and a brick wall covered with posters, an office chair sags like a marionette slumping in its box without an owner. Some newspaper and rags lay on the ground next to plastic bags and a boom box. I see all this as I walk and almost trip on the curb, split seconds between me and brushes into other people, a geometry of steps I take without thinking, a dance of avoiding one another so that we pass unscathed. Eyes and fingers on the tiny screens of cell phones where our faces scroll by, pixelated, captured. The lights of the city glow neon, phosphorescent like the moon when it's full and the clouds have no choice but to be bathed in mercury, that fluid fevers cannot hide from, pushed by our heat like electricity in the veins of each building; like waste and water in the pipes underneath us, pipes we walk over unaware, as we pass each other unaware, nearly kiss and kill and shove one another unaware of what or who we pass; or just what an empty chair might mean, what a passing glance could do to the world it takes in, world shaken by the sound of water gushing to the ground in smacks so much like the heavy rain in summer back in Texas during hurricane season, that slap of water loud, so it seems heavy, made of our skin it hurts to hear it, made of our faces we run into homes and away from that rushing, that rain hitting so hard it answers the thunder in a roar, in the collapsing of fists upon concrete, that

42

sound now to my right coming from the pay phone, from the man standing there, man who seems ruptured with his back to me; water pours from him in a flush like fireworks there in front of him; he stands shivering and groaning; the passing cars almost drown it out; the idle chatter and smacked gum and the chains on the purses slung on shoulders almost drown it out; the sound almost drowning with each passing foot, each step a knock on a door, the street fills up with the noise of people asking to come in, pounding and pounding like a heartbeat against the city where this man groans and I walk by, like you walk by, in this city where too much happens that nothing can happen, everyone going on with their lives, passing time, passing the empty thrones of each other's hearts, the empty place for each one of us in this city busy as the bloodstream in each of us.

Taken

In photos, my young father wears hats, gradually grows thinner as he loses his smile.

In one of the last ones taken, his moustache gleams like my black shoes and slicked hair in a photo taken on my first day of school.

Ocean Dream

In which I am pushed down into the sand only to look up and see a man running into the waves, his legs then breaking into waves, his body breaking into waves, something of my father's face breaking into waves, until all I am left with is that clash of water and sun that makes metaphor unnecessary.

Bukowski

A man on the radio reads you ranting about your stomach and rats gnawing at paper, those scraps that harbored you like the run-down room I stand in now, shaving, listening as the water runs, chorus to your words.

I slip when I hear that we will never be citizens of the world, that we are tied to our masterpieces as we are tied to hunger.

How did you say it to the cigarette? Did it ash and crumble? Did it flare in disbelief? Did the last bottle of wine knock over like a laugh too tired to sound, spilling into the corners of the room? Did you shrug it off, leave the mess to your typewriter, to another storm tapped into the night, keys clapping against paper like hail?

When your words finish in another man's voice, a thin ribbon of blood unfurls across my Adam's apple, bright with sunlight one second, dry like dust the next.

My history with the Spanish language

Something is offered up when we speak, and something is fed.

Mi familia es mi historia.

So it is that when I speak with family now, I take the time and say each word aware of how I may come across: a child making communion with all he knows.

Raro

¡Me dejaste con el corazón en la mano!

I hadn't heard my mother's voice in half a year. I wanted to say I forgot or lost track of something but that would have been too honest. I said instead that I had been busy, been good, been behaved, all of it in my best Spanish, which was in so many ways not saying much. With heart in hand, she began to tell me about my brothers, her graying hair, the silence her man needed in a small house.

¿No te levanta la mano, verdad? I asked, knowing that I would never trust the answer. *Cuidado con el descansito,* she said instead, then went on about how I am late with giving her grandchildren.

¿Qué haces? I told her I write poetry, my pages are my children. *Ni nada.* She then told me how a co-worker told her that I could write a book which could become a movie. Then I'll have money.

¿Qué piensas? This was my favorite question. I remember it from long drives at night, how she would say it as if she herself was tired of thinking. At that moment I had been thinking about how there were too many men in our family who take money, but how I always end up asking for some anyway.

Instead, I told her I'm the only Mexican writer in the workshop.

¿El único mexicano? I told her that I'm rare.

¿Raro? Raro tu nariz! And I laughed, and she laughed.

It went on that way, question and answer and advice, question and answer and silence, and it would go on that way, no matter how many sounds I threw out looking for the right one, we would always be like birds making as much of a home as we could out of broken things.

50

Section three

Old Love

When I dream of an old love, I let it ride, having already broken off what connected us, and not wanting to go through it all again. I drink my coffee the way they would remember me taking it, for some light and sweet, for others black and with a comment on how I can't believe how long it took me to take it this way, undiluted, untampered, bitter. With a heat on my tongue, I listen to old love, let my mind wander more than I did when I was with them, knowing I have had this conversation, feeling the answers give over as accommodating as leaves to sunlight. With a green on my tongue, I inevitably mix up the conversations: ask after the father of one whose father was never around; whisper an inside joke I realize too late I never shared. When old love looks at me lost, I ask, *Where did you get those,* and point sometimes to a set of bow and arrow earrings, sometimes a pair of toucans tattooed on the inside of an arm. Stories of boutiques I paced politely. Stories of a childhood fascination with colorful birds. *Don't you remember?* When we run out of small talk, I find myself pushing a baby carriage in which old love has fallen in. Helpless, I look down, only to hear myself doing baby talk, shaking my head, waving my hands, emphatically repeating words, and, in general, speaking in such a way I know I cannot ever make myself understood.

Degas

Watching a young couple walk in a bookstore, I remember young José trying to be slick, saying things like: *I level with poetry, then linger with prose.* Or: *Stay with me, love, the world is ours for the aching.*

So I said.

I'm still selfish. Still want to grab the couple by the hand, lead them to the Art section, heave a book of Degas into their hands, and ask them not to say anything stupid, to leave it to me.

I'd start with the ballerinas; say something about skin, the soft colors like smoke under moonlight. I'd tell them how it makes me shake with feeling the way the shading makes their faces almost not there. I would be in that shading, would be almost not here, have the edges fog into depth, background, perspective. But memory keeps on dabbing, keeps filling in, going over. I remember the stupid shit I'd say in rhyme – *I'm that Hispanic putting white girls in panic* – and reckoning – *You've made me a scapegoat to your incompetent heart.*

I would say I like Degas because his work shows you do not have to see something clearly to get a sense of it. Which is where they are, I realize. Young couple in a bookstore. Young couple I'm assuming too much of. Young signifier of my own past and signified conjectures. Two faces becoming two other faces, one of them my own, younger, then suddenly, and then irreversibly, still younger, but not mine anymore.

Sky Stone

The dense black curves of it round to the size of a lemon, and give not a reflection but a new face. He remembers the small hand holding it to his own face and being surprised at being lost. She kept referring to it as a sky stone – Not the blue, the later one. The one when stars are out and you can only see what they want you to: this is a piece of what they don't. A dark seed, he said then, and laughed, but didn't know why he was laughing, or why he had said what he said. As years pass, what else he could've said keeps passing. Each time he speaks it to himself at his desk, she doesn't laugh, only looks up at him as she did then, with eyes so clear the sky seems to be trapped there.

Books

After making the decision to leave my first wife, I remembered I had borrowed a copy of Peter S. Beagle's *The Last Unicorn* from a friend. I would turn from arguments, slammed doors, and long, cold February walks back to the paperback with yellowed pages, back to the butterfly quoting Yeats and riddles, to Schmendrick's bumbling magic, to the unicorn trying to imagine where the rest of her kind were.

When my ex threatened to have me deported, I found myself trying to trace back the stories I had told, about myself, about family struggles, what she might have confused or conjectured from things I was told not to share but shared anyway because I was in love. I looked up and only found her staring, laughing at my silence. I remember thinking briefly that her eyes were like the ocean in the story, the one where all the other unicorns were trapped inside of. For a long time after, I could not see waves as anything other than a trapped creature trying to break free.

I finished the book shortly after that. When I went to return it to my friend, she said that she herself had actually borrowed it from one of her brother's exes. I asked her to find the owner's address, and I mailed the book back with this note:

Often as I stand looking out across the water catching an image of the world and something of myself in it, a reflection true yet restless, moving with the wind and whatever rambles in the depths,

I wonder if this is what it feels like for books to have us poring over them, if they wonder at whatever invisible thing moves a face from concentrated stillness to sudden tears, sudden laughter, and if they think themselves human, feel in themselves something of the nature of the faces that see them.

I never heard back from the book's owner, and have no idea if my note meant anything. I do, though, often recall the cracks along the book's spine, and how I read the weathered pages knowing I wasn't the first to come across those words, that they were borrowed, like what makes up each breath.

Holiday Policy

My friend, who with his white beard and wide chest looks like Santa Claus, tells me of working at a liquor store and having to take Polaroids of people paying with a check. He did this when he was my age, but because I am my age, my friend becomes Santa with a camera and nametag, standing as straight as steel bars on windows, watching me buy my liquor. He laughs telling the story, but the Santa whose eyes are hard on me is silent. Under white eyebrows, I see myself already doubled, following the motions of the story: white flash; pen collapsing on the counter; bottles pointing fingers from brown paper bags; fluorescence hum below the words: *Holiday policy.* The photo hangs like a tongue out of the camera's mouth, my face slowly appearing from gray-white to a grainy, blurred reflection. *It was enough to put cash in their pockets, as if it had been there all along*, says my friend in the story, who himself dissolves into the friend in the room, grown quiet, as if he could hear himself speaking in the memory I would later have of him after he died, and disappointed that there isn't more to him than stories like this one.

59

Birthdays

Over breakfast, Ani reminds me it would be your birthday again today. I have been caught up in the smell of grass coming in from the window. The sharpness and warmth make me feel all this time before this moment I've been a stone hurled in the air, now nearing the horizon where from hereon it won't be seen.

> grass blades
> shift in the breeze
> moving the steam off my cup

At lunch, I try to recall things I haven't yet told Ani about you. Four years, and I haven't run out of words. What I do tell her about is people, those you would befriend and help out, scowl at and mistake for someone else, stories about cities you would've moved to if the time was right, the toys and books you collected, piled around your house, people waiting to hear from you, their pages and faces in place for later.

> palm-tree shadows
> on the stones
> of your uneven path

There is a side to the moon we never see. People are like

that, I tell Ani, pointing to myself. Her birthday was last week. I spent most of the day trying to make her laugh by saying things like: *Your laughter is popcorn to my soul.* The kind of things you say and hope the whole person hears them. What I wouldn't give to be able to reach and cup the side of the moon and turn it. When I imagine how it would go, I see a silver reflection of the hand I write with pull away, before it all flickers out.

> pen marks on this side of the page,
> on the other side
> impressions

Semblance

My aunt says she is glad I have my mother's eyes because it would have killed her to have run away from a man only to look down and see herself caught in the light of those eyes again.

My *Tía*'s Throw

after Roethke

In teaching the concept "wallowing in complexity," I tell my class I can say about my aunt: that I've gotten both my work ethic and sense of humor from her, as well as that she'd scold me by throwing whatever was in her hand.

I realize then, that I failed as a child, that instead of being punished with remote controls, bingo daubers, and sandals, I could've waited to act up when she was fluffing her pillow or buying cotton candy, could've made it easy on my body to incur her wrath as she washed her face or even scratched at lotto tickets, which she did with her thumbnail and would have resulted in my being pelted with shrivels of dust and a chance at big winnings.

I could've escaped sooner, been flung out of Texas one of the nights she came home from work, her hands swollen from rolling out tortillas, and reached down and wrapped her hand around mine so that a part of me disappeared in her fist.

In my squirming I could've told a lie, said a cuss word, looked at a dirty movie while no one was home, or dared to move her remote; could've stolen candy, started singing to myself down the grocery aisles, placed a dead cockroach on her newborn son's forehead, asked her where his father was and who, or said I didn't want to babysit; come home again with straight A's but a U in conduct – U for Unsatisfactory, which is what school called me when I'd speak out of turn, speak and keep speaking, not allowed to speak or make any noise too late at night or too early in the morning, and especially not in the afternoons when my aunt napped between shifts at two jobs.

In her fist I could've acted out, interrupted her laughter at my wincing by calling out *Lingo!* or *Ringo!* as I did in the Bingo hall, the old ladies down the long tables glaring behind cigarette smoke.

I could've done anything in her grip and been thrown like the salt shaker that one time through the window into the night sky, gotten lost much sooner, so she'd have to send someone else out into the yard to look for something that could never be found, that I swore then never landed, that perhaps is still shooting across the earth, which is impossible – I did listen in school – because if it was thrown and gone straight, it'd naturally go against the planet's curve and, after a while, enter into orbit, all the salt from our table scattered with the stars, which don't give enough light to see by but enough to glimpse the day I might act up and have her throw me at myself, defying logic, physics, and her, the day I'd soar far from the garage apartments and sleeping bags, far from report cards and chores, and land somewhere near this moment.

Letter to Rainer Maria Rilke from NYC

There cannot be this many people in the world – some have to be on repeat. Like the lady that just got off the train, I swear, we knew each other once, in fact, I am convinced she led me here to this city and now acts like I am no one, just to spite me.

These days, I spend my time in the parks or on the trains, always sitting. In this way, I feel I am everywhere. I am surprised I am not noticed. Once, I turned to no one in particular and read: *The blood of children runs through the streets/Like the blood of children.* That I can quote that without my skin splitting like fruit flesh means I am not scared anymore.

I like what you said about love, that it is pain, that it is joy.

I watch the rain fall in Times Square and cannot tell between the pixels and what drops and gathers on the ground in rags of light.

Solitude feels like fire sometimes.

Ready

Because I hear a hurried tone in my mother's voice. Because our conversation for years now doesn't last longer than ten minutes – the small talk of two changing shifts at a job. Because she explains how her ex (father of my oldest little brother) is on his way to fix the fuse box and her present boyfriend is going to be there to help. Because her ex was an electrician but had to have both of his arms cut off at the elbow after handling a live wire that cooked him at the hands. Because those hands dragged my mother down stone steps into the backyard when he lived with us. Because he hit her often in those days, before and after his son was around. Because I was a child and heard first, saw later the steps dark as my mother's face. Because he only stopped when our neighbor ran over, pulled the ex off her and said *My wife's calling the police just stop.* Because he'd yell at her in the bedroom with the music loud: the television, the bedframe, the vanity, the very earth rattled like the sides of a cage. Because this man can still see, still has everything he knows about how to make a living, can guide anyone in how to move their hands properly to fix what is wrong with the breakers. Because her present boyfriend is a quiet man, an understanding man (or so I've been told and try to see in photos she sends of family vacations: her smiling, him around my other two brothers from another father). Because she keeps stopping mid-sentence, and in those pauses I hear the opening and closing of doors, the shuffling through the closet past a dress that hasn't been moved in years and perhaps has only shifted from when she was last pushed against it. Because she keeps picking up the conversation by saying she has to get the house ready. Because I wonder what there is to get ready: something is broken and will stay broken no matter how nice everything around it is made. Because I grew up sharing a room with my mother, seeing her get ready for work or to go out, all that attention paid on herself (not to herself) second nature. Because I have watched birds come back to specific trees across summers, day after day, with the same detached focus and flutter. Because I am no longer there for her to ask me how she looks. Because I wonder when the last time she asked me was and can't place it. Because she has tried to end the call three times now and three times gotten caught up in saying various goodbyes, as well as making plans for our next conversation, which is in itself a constant topic of conversation between us—I decide I gotta go, I love her, I see she's busy, I just wanted to hear how she is.

Traffic

Like the fall of snowflakes one cannot keep track of and lets fall one after another giving them all the same name – *snow* – to winter what leaves are to a tree, a passing presence – these faces driving by, strained and focused in their lives, one after another, pass, unaware of this ceremony, this dedication, this kingdom.

Song

If you have ever watched someone fall to sleep, seen fluttered eyes still, hands writhe until even the mouth gives over its natural grimace, forfeits shape – as the complex web of a spider slacks to simple thread – then perhaps you could name the song that rings in the silence of all the worry and desire that until moments ago seemed so driven and unending.

Slowed

Sometimes the garbage in our apartment gets to being piled up so each new thing rises. Other things have been on my mind. Do you remember when we worked at a Starbucks together? First day we met, you were all sun and a tank-top. You weren't on the clock. I was. You had just been transferred and come in to introduce yourself to the crew, perhaps to size us up. Come to think of it, I never asked why you came in. That question is lost under everything else that came in with you. That sun I spoke about in your hair, the brown flecked with light. I was pissed, just about to clock out, but in you came. The guy who would take over for me stopped and chatted with you, stood in my way. I was tired. I had an unruly woman to go home to then. She hated when I was home late. I heard your name. And that got lost too, at first. That sun in your hair and a mouth that wasn't smiling when I looked up. I remembered then I had my nametags in my hand. Instead of saying one word to you, I raised them, waved my name before you like twin birds or the way police would show photos of people they hope you could identify. You told me later you thought me slow after that first impression. Perhaps I was, not slow, but slowed. For that sun in your hair. The garbage can wait a little longer.

Don't Shoot Me

Place recipes for fudge or prayers of courage and resignation of ancient Greek warriors on the inside front and back covers. Sketch a treasure map across the flyleaf. Leave clues to forgotten mysteries in the margins and footnotes on the bottom detailing the telephone directory of whatever zip code my book is being sold in at that time. Let people have choices: after a poem, let the reader consider whether it would be best for the poet to climb into the submarine and pursue the pirates in secret (turn to page 26), or to strap on his jetpack and blast across the Gulf of Mexico only to be confused for a comet, pointed and gawked at by the city folk of Corpus Christi, and later dedicated to the memory of Selena, patron saint of sequin studded hips (turn to page 30).

Just don't shoot me.

Don't force a wholesome smile from me against a wooded backdrop. Don't catch me by surprise, my back to a brick wall, in black and white, looking off into the distance. Don't make me mad or sad or whatever it is that makes writers stare directly into the camera with that vague blend of intensity and impatience, as if they were in an art museum staring down a painting and lingering in that spot long enough for patient appreciation to turn into defiance, stiffness protracted into silent proclamation as if saying – I get you, I get you, I am deep and I understand and I deeply understand and no art is better than me, nuh-uh, no way.

If you must, at least keep me hip. Work out a deal where I can replace the photo on the jacket with a sticker of a new me. A new me that in 1992 would've worn flannel and gone unshaven. In 1997, poppin' the collar of a shiny suit a la Puff Daddy. In 2004, in a throwback next to an Escalade with rims the size of small children. In 2010, watching *Lost* episodes on my phone. At least that way, I won't be in some suit and tie, with a hat, when we no longer wear hats in 2025 because of the cyber-helmets we have to use that allow us to communicate through telepathy.

As you can tell, I'm thinking in terms of the future. I'm thinking you won't want to see me later. I'm thinking it'll never happen. I'm thinking – you won't like what I'm thinking.

Because if you put me through it, if you make me stand silent and still, sweating as the crook of your finger triggers all the decisions, chooses for me what there is to recall of my face, you know what I'll be thinking?

I'll be thinking of your mother. Your mother under the sycamore trees. Your mother against a brick wall. Your mother in a museum, deep and understood. Your mother in '92, threshed in flannel. Your mother in '97 with her collar popped. Your mother in my Escalade. Your mother on my phone laughing when Jack screams out: *We have to go back!*

The look on my face won't be me, intense or deep. Won't be me, with a grin the size of a sycamore's widest branches. That look will be me, 2025, will be telepathy, from me to you: I am a literary lion, and I hate taking pictures.

Moth Season

Inspector Moth walked from one end of the brightness to the other. Still, the pane remained. He had crashed into it not knowing why. He paced, tapping at the glass now and then, boxing with his reflection, the colors he was made of pushing back. The whole world, he thought, can see that I am stuck.

§ § §

Behind neon signs and their blinking letters. In the corner of the ceiling where a hook hangs down and a cobweb shags. In the corner of the floor with dried leaves and the pollen from the cottonwoods. Under the sink where the stiff bodies of roaches are unfortunate and in the way. Behind the newspapers stacked outside where even he lost track of himself amidst the gray and the words – Inspector Moth looked everywhere for a clue.

§ § §

This time of night he couldn't go outside, it wasn't safe. So many looked like him. And the heat. He almost lost himself. What was he doing against the screen door, shaking the sides of his trench coat again? What was he feeling, rolling skittering on the sidewalk, his newspaper wings unfolding and folding? Who was he that he couldn't solve this case, couldn't even remember it, could only watch himself and watch himself and watch himself?

§ § §

Inspector Moth knew there was something he had to do. He ruffled through the pockets of his trench coat, flung the damn thing around trying to get it off. The coat would not leave his body. He took a few steps around the office. His trench coat billowed around him. There was something he had to do.

§ § §

Inspector Moth's list of suspects: the screen door, the branches letting leaves fall, a tangle of stray hairs, all colors of confetti, feathers, lost buttons holding nothing together, lost earrings looking dangerous and guilty, wood grain surfaces where even he could hide, tomorrow, light.

§ § §

She walked into his life like the flick of a light switch, from darkness to bright. She was something he had not factored in, something he had to adjust to. First, his eyes. He had grown used to being alone, to silence like a second self-holding its tongue. Now there was her. Her hair the color of sunlight on paint. Her voice that cracked into him like the wind knocking into and through a cicada shell, words of grit, gust, shame: *What is that dirty butterfly doing here?*

§ § §

Inspector Moth's list of things he has mistaken for the moon: aspirin tablets (like two moons split before a glass of water), headlights (which did the unthinkable and flew toward him), a desk lamp (where a man sat writing down what the moon had to say), table tops in an empty restaurant (a room made of moons), the crown of an old man waiting on a corner at night (the moon shaking as he lost his step), an empty parking lot where the streetlamps had given out (the face of a still lake), manhole covers on an empty street (the footprints of the moon), empty dryers (moons whose faces opened and he climbed inside).

§ § §

Flag, stop mocking my wings. Store sign on your chains, stop mocking my wings. Red dress hanging off a chair, stop mocking my wings. Empty sleeves on a clothes line, stop mocking my wings. Curtains closing and opening in the wind, stop mocking my wings. Pages flurred in the book on the table, stop mocking my wings. Leaves behind me in the night, stop mocking my wings. Water down there in the stream, stop mocking my wings. Clouds moving, always moving, stop mocking my wings.

77

78

NOTES

Forgotten Conversation: While the stolen book in question in this piece was a review copy of Sandra Cisneros' *Caramelo,* the phrase *juntito a mí* is taken from the Cisneros poem "Dulzura" from her collection *Loose Woman.*

Concrete: The epigraph comes from Carl Dennis' book *Meetings With Time.* I wrote the first draft of this piece at the age of twenty-five, when the borrowed lines rang true for me.

Verisimilitude: This piece is an adaptation of one of the Irish folktales W. B. Yeats speaks of in his book *The Celtic Twilight.*

Jalapeños: The phrasing of *When I am old and gray* is a reference to W. B. Yeats' short lyric "When You Are Old and Grey."

Bukowski: This poem was inspired by Garrison Keillor's reading of Charles Bukowski's "a place in Philly" on The Writer's Almanac.

Holiday Policy & Birthdays: These pieces were written in memory of my friend Dennis Flinn (1948-2010), Corpus Christi poet and friend to many.

My Tia's Throw: This piece is an homage of sorts to Theodore Roethke's famous poem "My Papa's Waltz."

Letter to Rainer Maria Rilke from NYC: This piece was written in the spirit of Rainer Maria Rilke's famous *Letters to a Young Poet.* The line: *The blood of children runs through the streets/ Like the blood of children,* is my own rough translation of a line from Pablo Neruda's poem "*Explico Algunas Cosas.*"

Acknowledgments

Special thanks to the editors of the following publications where the works noted were published:

Hanging Loose – Directions

Tahoma Literary Review – Spiderman Hitches a Ride

Right Hand Pointing – Love Dream, Zoot Suit Riot

Contemporary Haibun Online – Walks, Birthdays

Blue Mesa Review – Don't Look Now I Might Be Mexican (3rd place, 2014 Poetry contest)

Apogee/Perigree Blog – Forgotten Conversation

The Fox Chase Review – Childhood

cur.ren.cy – Bombs, Morning Communion

Star 82 Review – 5 a.m.

Pretty Owl Poetry – Stream

Compose: A Journal of Simply Good Writing - Raro

The Acentos Review – Letter to Rainer Maria Rilke from NYC

Cactus Heart – Moth Season

Ocean Dream and *Concrete* were previously published as part of the poetry chapbook *The Wall* (Tiger's Eye Press, 2012).

82

Made in the USA
Middletown, DE
18 December 2015